GREAT OUTDOORS
SPORTS ZONE

SMALL GAME
HUNTING
RABBIT, RACCOON, SQUIRREL,
OPOSSUM, AND MORE

by Tom Carpenter

Lerner Publications Company • Minneapolis

Lerner Publications Company
A division of Lerner Publishing Group, Inc.
241 First Avenue North
Minneapolis, MN 55401 U.S.A.

Website address: www.lernerbooks.com

Content Consultant: James G. Dickson, PhD, wildlife biologist, researcher, author, professor, and hunter

Library of Congress Cataloging-in-Publication Data
Carpenter, Tom, 1962-
    Small game hunting : rabbit, raccoon, squirrel, opossum, and more / by Tom Carpenter.
      p. cm. — (Great outdoors sports zone)
    Includes index.
    ISBN 978–1–4677–0224–9 (lib. bdg. : alk. paper)
    1. Small game hunting—Juvenile literature. I. Title.
SK340.C37 2013
799.2'5—dc23   2012002264

Manufactured in the United States of America
1 – CG – 7/15/12

The images in this book are used with the permission of: Backgrounds: © Mackey Creations/Shutterstock Images; © iraladybird/Shutterstock Images; © Jason Derry/iStockphoto; © Ryan Kelly/iStockphoto, p. 5; © Library of Congress, pp. 6 (LC-USZ62-51139), 8 (top) (LC-USZC2-2954), 9 (LC-DIG-nclc-01498); © David Parsons/iStockphoto, p. 7; © Paul Moore/Bigstock, p. 8 (bottom); © USBFCO/Shutterstock Images, p. 11 (top); © Evoken/Shutterstock Images, p. 11 (bottom); © John and Karen Hollingsworth/USFWS , pp. 12, 13; © Nate A./Shutterstock Images, p. 15 (top); © Sascha Burkard/Shutterstock Images, p. 15 (bottom); © Sari Oneal/Shutterstock Images, p. 16; © StudioNewmarket/Shutterstock Images, p. 17; © Richard Goerg/iStockphoto, p. 18 (top); © Dennis Steen/Shutterstock Images, p. 18 (bottom); © Risteski Goce/Shutterstock Images, pp. 19 (top), 20 (top); © Volodymyr Krasyuk/Shutterstock Images, p. 19 (bottom); © Willee Cole/Shutterstock Images, p. 20 (bottom left); © kostrez/Shutterstock Images, p. 20 (bottom right); © dcwcreations/Shutterstock Images, p. 21; © Tyler Olson/iStockphoto, p. 22 (top); © Red Line Editorial, pp. 22 (bottom), 24 (top), 25 (middle), 28 (bottom), 29 (top); © Uldis Austrins/Shutterstock Images, p. 23; © Nekrasov Andrey/Shutterstock Images, p. 24 (bottom); © Alucard2100/Shutterstock Images, p. 25 (top); © Brian Lasenby/Shutterstock Images, p. 26 (top); © James M Phelps, Jr/Shutterstock Images, p. 26 (middle); © Frank Doyle/USFWSm p. 26 (bottom); © nialat/Shutterstock Images, p. 27 (top); © Ultrashock/Shutterstock Images, p. 27 (middle); © Adam Larsen/iStockphoto, p. 27 (bottom); © ason/Shutterstock Images, p. 29 (bottom).
Front cover: © BillMarchel.com; Background © iStockphoto.com/Marcin Kowalski.

Main body text set in Avenir LT Std 65 Medium 11/17.
Typeface provided by Adobe Systems.

TABLE OF CONTENTS

CHAPTER ONE

WHY HUNT SMALL GAME?

Hunting small game is a great way to start your hunting career. Squirrels, opossums, raccoons, rabbits, and hare are all small game. Some of these wild animals are hunted for food.

Small game are usually easy to find if you are hunting in the right habitat. A habitat is where an animal lives. This area includes shelter and food for the animal. Most small game live in woods and fields.

Hiking to find small game is good exercise. And this activity is a fun way to spend time with an older friend or family member. Many of the places to hunt small game are beautiful too.

Hunting small game takes good shooting skills. The game hide well and make little targets. A hunter needs to get close enough for a shot. But the targets move fast! The animals might be little, but small game hunting is big fun!

Small game hunting is an exciting sport that takes place across North America.

CHAPTER TWO

HISTORY OF SMALL GAME HUNTING

Native Americans were the first small game hunters in North America. Rabbits and squirrels were important to their survival. Native Americans relied on hunting for food. The game provided meat and furs. Many groups had great respect for the game they killed.

Learning to hunt small game was important for young Native Americans. Adults hunted bigger game such as deer. But boys and girls improved their skills by hunting squirrels and rabbits.

Young Native Americans learned to shoot bows and arrows by hunting small game.

Native American rock art shows that early hunters relied on both big and small game to feed their families.

These young shooters hunted with bows and arrows. They would stalk, or sneak up on, a squirrel or a rabbit and then hit that small target with an arrow. They learned to hunt quietly and shoot accurately. Some hunters used a kind of dart thrower called an atlatl for small game. Native Americans also used traps and snares to catch squirrels and rabbits.

Early American hunters used traps to catch small game animals in the 1800s.

European Hunters

When European settlers came to the United States in the 1500s and the 1600s, they also relied on small game for food. These early settlers used flintlock rifles for hunting. These old-fashioned rifles loaded through the muzzle, or front end. Great skill was needed to shoot small game with a flintlock rifle. The settlers also trapped rabbits and other small game for their meat and fur.

Flintlock rifle

When settlers arrived, some of their practices helped rabbit populations increase. Farmers cleared land and created sunny openings in the forests. As a result, brush areas became more common. And these spots were ideal rabbit habitats. Rabbit populations grew through the 1800s and peaked in the 1920s and the 1930s.

Modern game management and hunting regulations have made plenty of small game available to hunt. Large forests and small woodlands hold squirrels. Rabbits live in brushy areas. Raccoons can be found almost everywhere. With the right tools and skills, you can hunt small game like the Native Americans and early settlers did!

In the early 1900s, this South Carolina boy hunted rabbits to eat or sell in town.

PROTECTING
SMALL GAME

It's important to protect animals so future hunters can enjoy small game hunting too. State fish and game agencies are responsible for managing game populations. Protecting habitats for these animals is the biggest concern of these agencies. Animals need a good habitat for hiding from predators, feeding, raising young, and surviving winter and other hard times.

Habitat

Every animal species has different habitat needs. Squirrels need mature woodlands. These are older forests with large trees. Squirrels like nut trees, such as oak, hickory, walnut, and beech. Squirrels also like to be near fields of farm crops such as corn. This makes food easy to find.

Rabbits often like areas of low, thick plant cover. This includes land that has been logged, farmed, burned, or otherwise disturbed and left to grow back wild. In this brushland, rabbits can find places to hide. Rabbits also like to be near open land such as meadows and farm fields.

Look for squirrels in areas where there are mature trees.

Raccoons and opossums can live almost anywhere. They just need places for hiding, such as forested land or garbage cans. You might even see a raccoon in the middle of a city!

When habitats are healthy, small game populations grow large. Hunters can take more animals because the habitat has more animals than it can support. But often, limits are placed on hunters to make sure they don't take too many animals.

You can find raccoons almost anywhere. Make sure the area is safe and legal for hunting before you start shooting.

11

A biologist sets a trap for a fox squirrel. Biologists study small game to set hunting rules.

Hunting Seasons and Bag Limits

Biologists are scientists who study living things. Some biologists focus on game animals and populations. These scientists set rules, such as hunting seasons and bag limits. These rules help hunters enjoy the outdoors without harming wild-animal populations. These efforts result in conservation, or the responsible use of natural resources.

Hunting seasons occur when animals are done having their offspring for the year and their babies can survive on their own.

Many animals give birth in the spring, so most small game hunting happens in the fall or winter. The cooler weather also means game meat is less likely to spoil in the field. Bag limits are created so that no hunter shoots more than his or her share of game in a single day.

All states require a hunter to buy a hunting license. The license says what kind of game the hunter can hunt. The licenses help fish and game agencies keep track of who is hunting what game. States set limits on the number of licenses for animal species that have small populations. This protects that animal from being overhunted. The money made from buying hunting licenses supports game departments and their work in conservation.

An official from the U.S. Fish and Wildlife Service checks a hunter's license. Hunters can be fined for hunting without a license.

CHAPTER FOUR

BE A SAFE HUNTER

Hunting is a big responsibility. But there are many hunting laws and practices that will help you have fun and stay safe.

Safety Training

Most states require young hunters to take firearms or hunting safety classes. In a safety class, you will learn how to hunt smart so that you don't injure yourself or a fellow hunter.

MENTORED HUNTING

Many states offer mentored hunting programs to give young people a chance to try hunting before committing to a safety class. A mentor is an experienced, licensed hunter who teaches you about hunting and safety while out in the field. A mentor might be an older family member or friend.

Hunting alongside an experienced adult hunter is a great way to learn about the sport.

Places to Hunt

All state game agencies list public hunting lands on their websites. Public hunting lands might be wildlife management areas, county and state forests, or federal land. Hunters should not hunt on land if they are unsure if it is public.

You can have a lot of hunting success on private land. It is your responsibility to ask permission to hunt on private land and know the boundaries of the land. Never hunt on private land without permission.

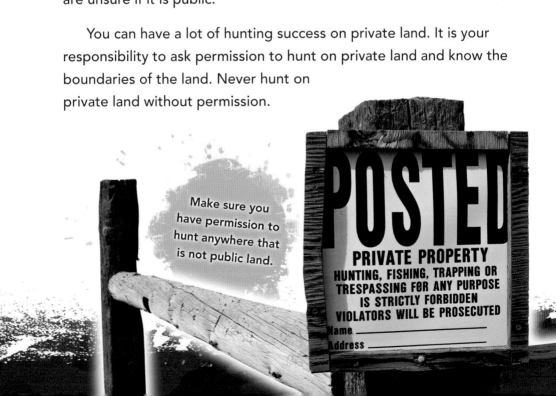

Make sure you have permission to hunt anywhere that is not public land.

POSTED
PRIVATE PROPERTY
HUNTING, FISHING, TRAPPING OR
TRESPASSING FOR ANY PURPOSE
IS STRICTLY FORBIDDEN
VIOLATORS WILL BE PROSECUTED
Name _____
Address _____

States have rules about how late in the evening you can legally shoot. Shooting in poor light can be dangerous.

Hunting Regulations

Each state publishes its hunting regulations. You need to know and follow these rules. Not knowing a law is not an excuse for breaking it! You can find regulations booklets at sporting goods stores, state offices, or online at your state's fish and game agency website.

Some of the key regulations to know include these:

Hunting season dates: Make sure the season is open before you go hunting!

Shooting times: Good light is needed when shooting. Find out when it is legal to shoot in the morning and how late shooting is allowed in the evening.

Bag limits: Different small game have different limits for how many animals can be taken in a day.

Blaze orange: Most states require hunters to wear a blaze-orange cap and a certain amount of other blaze-orange clothing while hunting. This keeps other hunters from confusing people with animals.

Fair Chase

Good hunters follow a code of ethics beyond what is in a regulations booklet. Acting ethically means doing what is right even when others are not watching. This means hunting in a way that is fair to the animal and other hunters.

Good ethics include hunting with fair chase methods. For example, don't shoot into squirrel nests or at helpless young animals. If you do kill an animal, make its death as quick and painless as possible. Work hard to locate the game you shot. Make the most of your game meat.

BLAZE ORANGE

Your state may require you to wear blaze-orange-colored clothing. Even if it's not the law, wearing blaze orange is a good idea. This might include an orange-colored cap, hunting vest, or jacket. There is no color in nature like neon blaze orange. Hunting accidents can happen when one hunter confuses another hunter with a moving animal. But wearing this bright color makes hunters visible to other hunters.

Blaze-orange clothing helps you stand out from your natural surroundings.

LET'S GO HUNTING!

It's almost time to go hunting! But first, you need to know what gear you need. Then you will need to learn the techniques for hunting different small game.

Guns for Small Game

The most popular firearm for hunting small game is a .22 caliber rifle. Caliber is the diameter, or distance across the rifle's inside barrel. This is the long part that fits the bullet. The cartridge includes a small case containing powder and the bullet.

.22 caliber
rifle

.22 caliber
cartridge

FIREARMS SAFETY

Remember these letters: **TAB-K**. It is the basic formula for gun safety.

- **T**reat every firearm as if it were loaded.
- **A**lways point the muzzle away from people.
- **B**e sure of your target and what lies beyond it.
- **K**eep the safety on (to prevent accidental firing) and your finger off the trigger until you are ready to fire.

Some hunters use 20-gauge shotguns for small game. The gauge is the measurement of the inside diameter of the barrel. A 20-gauge shotgun is loaded with a shell and a case that holds powder and shot pellets. When a hunter fires the shell, the pellets spread out and hit the game.

20-gauge shotgun

Shotgun shell and pellets

Other Small Game Hunting Equipment

Here are a few other items that might come in handy for hunting small game.

Scope

A scope is a small telescope that attaches to the barrel of your gun to help you spot and aim at game. You can put a scope on a .22 caliber rifle. The scope will be very accurate to about 35 yards (32 meters).

Boots

Hunting usually involves some hiking, so wear boots that fit well and are suited to the weather.

A scope will help you shoot with more accuracy.

Comfortable, sturdy boots are important when hunting in woods or fields.

Carry a hunting knife to help in field dressing game.

Most small game hunting takes place in cool weather, so make sure you dress warmly.

Hunting Coat or Vest

Blaze orange is the best color. Your coat or vest should have a game bag or pocket for carrying game.

Hat and Gloves

Wear an orange hat that will keep your head warm and visible. A cap with a wide brim will help keep the sun out of your eyes. Gloves will keep your hands warm in cold weather.

Knife

Removing an animal's internal organs as soon as possible keeps the meat safe to eat. This is called field dressing. A small knife is important for field dressing game.

If you're rabbit hunting in the winter, look for tracks in the snow.

Now that you are geared up, it's time to hit the hunting grounds!

Hunting Rabbits

Front feet

Back feet

RABBIT AND HARE TRACKS

Most rabbit hunting is done on the move. Walk through brushy areas and kick at brush piles and tall grass. Look for evidence of rabbits, such as tracks or droppings. Pay attention! Rabbits are fast and quiet. When a rabbit flushes, or runs from its hiding spot, get ready to shoot. The rabbit might freeze and give you a good chance for a shot. You also might be able to get a shot as the rabbit bounds away. This tests your shooting skills.

Hare are related to rabbits but are slightly larger. In northern states and mountain areas, many hunters pursue snowshoe hare in winter. This is challenging because snowshoe hare are white against a background of white snow. To hunt snowshoe hare, walk quietly through wooded areas and fields looking for a hare's black eyes or ear tips.

Beagles and basset hounds make good rabbit dogs. When a rabbit is flushed, the dogs will trail the rabbit. A rabbit often stays in an area it knows well, so wait in the spot you first saw the rabbit. When you hear your dogs turn and start heading back toward you, get ready!

Beagles make great rabbit dogs.

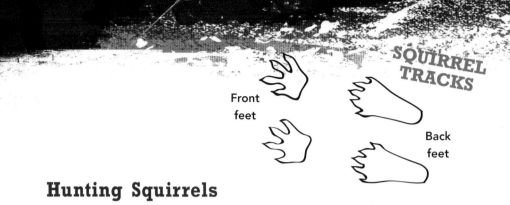

Front feet

Back feet

Hunting Squirrels

Squirrel hunting is a great way to start small game hunting because squirrels are often easy to find. When hunting for squirrels, listen for them in the leaves or tree branches. Keep an eye out for a tail hanging over a tree limb or an odd bump on a branch. If a squirrel is hiding behind a tree, try throwing a stick on that side. A squirrel might scurry to your side. One way to hunt for squirrels is to walk slowly through the woods until you spot one. Then slowly move into position for a shot. You can also hunt squirrels with the help of a dog. A good squirrel dog hunts through the woods until it sees or smells a squirrel. Then the dog trails the squirrel and chases it up a tree. This is called treeing a squirrel. The dog will bark and guard the tree until you arrive.

A dog's help can make your hunt more successful—and more fun!

Night hunting is exciting. Shine a light in the woods or a field and you just might see an opossum staring back at you.

Hunting Raccoons and Opossums

Most raccoon and opossum hunting is done at night with the aid of flashlights and spotlights. This is legal in most places because raccoons and opossums are most active at night. One way to hunt raccoons and opossums is to walk along forest or farm field edges. As you go, shine a spotlight into fields and trees. Look for a feeding raccoon or opossum. You might see the game's shiny eyes reflecting back at you. Another way to hunt is with coonhounds. When a dog smells a raccoon, it follows the scent to the raccoon. It chases the raccoon until it climbs a tree. Then the coonhound barks at the tree, trapping the raccoon until you come with a spotlight and take a shot.

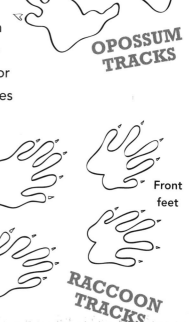

Front feet

Back feet

OPOSSUM TRACKS

Front feet

Back feet

RACCOON TRACKS

SMALL GAME GUIDE

GRAY SQUIRREL

Gray squirrels weigh about 1 pound (0.5 kilograms). They live in both sprawling forests and small, isolated woods. Look for gray squirrel nests built of leaves in V-shaped tree forks. Watch for cracked nutshells on the ground where squirrels feed. Listen for squirrels' cackling calls.

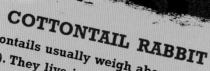

FOX SQUIRREL

Fox squirrels weigh about 2 pounds (0.9 kg). They make their homes in open woods and small groups of trees. Look for nests and tree holes with entrances worn white and smooth by squirrels. Check stumps for nutshells. Look for corncobs dragged into the woods.

COTTONTAIL RABBIT

Cottontails usually weigh about 3 pounds (1.3 kg). They live in overgrown areas, brushy thickets, berry patches, bush piles, hedgerows, and grassy, abandoned fields. Look for rabbit tracks in the snow and rabbit trails in the grass.

SNOWSHOE HARE

Snowshoe hare weigh about 4 pounds (1.7 kg). They live in the far north and in high mountain areas. Snowshoes are brown in summer, but they turn white in winter! Good snowshoe hare habitats are brushy thickets, swamps, and forests that are young and dense with small trees. Look for hare tracks in the snow or gnawed bark where hare have fed.

RACCOON

Raccoons usually weigh between 4 and 23 pounds (1.7 and 10 kg). Raccoons can thrive in almost any kind of habitat, including woodlands, wetlands, farmland, prairies, cities, or mountains. Raccoons like being near water. Look for raccoon tracks in the mud along creeks.

OPOSSUM

Opossums weigh between 3 and 13 pounds (1.3 and 5.9 kg). They move very slowly. Like raccoons, opossums can live most anywhere. Look for opossum tracks in the mud. An opossum's back-foot track almost looks like a small human handprint.

SMALL GAME CARE, CLEANING, AND COOKING

Part of your responsibility as a hunter is to eat what you shoot. Fortunately, small game taste great! But to have delicious meals, you must properly care for your game in the field, clean it well, and know how to cook it.

Field Care

When you shoot small game, you should clean your game as soon as possible. You can improve the quality of your meat by field dressing the animal. This cools down the animal more quickly, which keeps the meat from going bad. As a bonus, your game is lighter to carry.

ADULT HELP NEEDED!

Because you'll be using a sharp knife and working with raw meat, get help from an experienced hunter when you are cleaning and cooking small game!

How to Skin a Rabbit

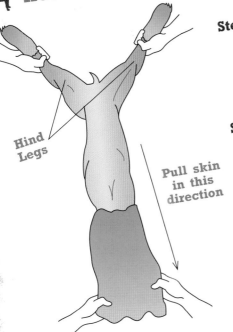

Hind Legs

Pull skin in this direction

Step 1
Have a partner hold the rabbit up by its hind (back) legs.

Step 2
Pull the skin off from the back of the rabbit to the front (top to bottom).

Step 3
Use a knife to cut off the rabbit's feet and head.

Cooking Small Game

One great way to cook small game is to fry it. Roll the meat in flour or a seasoned coating. Heat ½ inches (1 centimeter) of vegetable oil or bacon drippings in a skillet. Fry the meat until it is fully cooked. The meat should be sizzling or smoking and hot all the way through. Most chicken recipes will also work well for cooking small game.

Hunting rabbit and other small game is worth the hard work.

GLOSSARY

BAG LIMIT

the maximum number of animals of a species a hunter can kill in a day

CONSERVATION

the thoughtful, efficient, and careful use of natural resources

ETHICS

the way a hunter acts in the field that is fair to the animals and the sport

HABITAT

the place an animal lives, which provides the animal with hiding, food sources, and water

NATURAL RESOURCES

things found in nature that are useful for humans

OFFSPRING

the young of an animal or a human

RIFLE

a long-barreled gun that shoots a single bullet

SAFETY

a device on a firearm that keeps it from accidentally firing

SHOTGUN

a long-barreled gun that shoots pellets that spread out

SPECIES

animals that are grouped together by scientists because they are related

FOR MORE INFORMATION

Further Reading

Fleisher, Paul. *Forest Food Webs*. Minneapolis: Lerner Publications Company, 2008.

Landau, Elaine. *Beagles Are the Best!* Minneapolis: Lerner Publications Company, 2010.

MacRae, Sloan. *Small-Game Hunting: Rabbits, Squirrels, and Other Small Animals*. New York: PowerKids Press, 2011.

Websites

Boys' Life Animal Tracks Identification Quiz
http://boyslife.org/hobbies-projects/funstuff/6662/animal-track-identification-quiz/
Take a quiz to see how much you know about animal tracks. Then use what you learned when you go hunting!

Junior Shooters
http://www.juniorshooters.net/
This website features information on hunting clubs, events, and safety geared toward young shooters.

U.S. Fish and Wildlife Service: Hunting
http://www.fws.gov/hunting/
This website has information on conservation, national hunting regulations, and resources on where to go to learn the hunting rules for your own state.

INDEX

About the Author

Tom Carpenter has hunted and fished across North America for almost five decades, pursuing big game, waterfowl, upland birds, wild turkeys, small game, and fish of all kinds. He has raised three sons as sportsmen and written countless articles and contributed to dozens of books on hunting, fishing, nature, and the outdoors.